100 Masterpieces in the Van Gogh Museum

A selection by director John Leighton

Contents

Foreword

The Van Gogh Museum in Amsterdam houses the world's largest collection of works by Vincent van Gogh as well as a substantial number of paintings, drawings, prints and sculptures by other artists of the 19th century. In the relatively short period since it was first opened in 1973 as a permanent home for the collections of the Vincent van Gogh Foundation, the museum has become a hugely popular institution. Each year over a million visitors from all over the globe pass through our doors.

With more than two hundred paintings, five hundred drawings, and a substantial archive that includes some seven hundred of Van Gogh's letters, the museum is not only a place of pilgrimage for the enthusiast but a seemingly limitless resource for the detailed study of the artist and his era. A visit to the Van Gogh Museum affords the unique opportunity to follow almost every twist and turn in the artist's brief career, from his first hesitant exercises in a sombre realism through to the resplendent colour of his last works. And these pictures are not seen in isolation but as part of an unfolding history of avant-garde art in the 19th century and early 20th century in which Vincent's works can be viewed alongside works by the leading artists of his time.

A number of the paintings illustrated here are recent acquisitions. In its efforts to improve the quality of its collection, the Van Gogh Museum has been fortunate to enjoy extraordinarily generous support from sponsors and benefactors including the Vereniging Rembrandt; the Nationaal Fonds Kunstbezit; the Mondriaan Stichting; the VSB-Fonds; and Sara Lee Corporation. The Van Gogh Museum is one of four national museums that receives funds from the Sponsor Bingo Lottery and this support has greatly enhanced our purchasing power in recent years.

This book is designed to reflect the very special character of the collections at the Van Gogh Museum. The selection of one hundred masterworks includes many of Van Gogh's major paintings as well as representative pictures by friends and contemporaries such as Monet, Toulouse-Lautrec or Gauguin. The accompanying texts are brief in order to allow full play to the illustrations of the pictures. I hope that you will enjoy this introduction to the collection and that it might inspire you to visit (or revisit) the museum itself to view these extraordinary works of art at first hand.

John Leighton

The museum and collection

Wheatfield under thunderclouds [73]

The Van Gogh Museum opened in 1973. The collection, on loan from the Vincent van Gogh Foundation, comprises more than 200 paintings, 500 drawings, four sketchbooks and around 700 letters by Van Gogh. The museum also displays works by Vincent's contemporaries which the artist and his brother Theo van Gogh (1857–1891) bought or acquired through exchanges.

A number of years ago the museum adopted a supplementary purchasing and exhibition policy. As well as presenting its own Van Gogh collection, the emphasis now lies on the acquisition and display of Western, mainly French, art from the period 1840–1920.

The museum has evolved into an institution which exhibits European art from the second half of the nineteenth century and first decades of the twentieth century, with works by leading French artists such as Claude Monet (1840–1926), Paul Gauguin (1848–1903), Georges Seurat (1859–1891), Pierre Puvis de Chavannes (1824–1898) and Odilon Redon (1840–1916).

History

Although the museum is comparatively young, its collection has enjoyed a long history. Van Gogh's works originally belonged to Theo, Vincent's younger brother, who worked for the Paris art dealers Goupil & Co. (later Boussod, Valadon & Cie.) in Paris. From the start of his career as an artist Vincent sent the majority of his works to Theo in exchange for the latter's moral and financial support.

After Theo's death in 1891 the collection legally passed to his son Vincent Willem van Gogh (1890–1978); however, Theo's widow

The interior of the museum, Rietveld building

Johanna van Gogh-Bonger (1862–1925) would act as administrator of the collection until her death. She returned to The Netherlands, where she did everything in her power to promote Vincent's work, initiating exhibitions and selling pictures from the collection.

Thanks to Johanna's efforts Van Gogh's genius gained international recognition during the second decade of the 20th century. At this point she decided to keep the rest of the collection together and rarely sold any works after 1920.

When Johanna died in 1925 her son Vincent Willem assumed responsibility for the collection. In 1930 he decided to lend the majority of the works to the Stedelijk Museum in Amsterdam, largely at the prompting of his wife, Josina van Gogh-Wibaut (1891–1933),

who thought it was a pity that the public was unable to enjoy the many Van Gogh paintings in the family collection.

Vincent Willem van Gogh, also known as 'the Engineer' (he was a mechanical engineer by profession) initially kept his distance from his uncle's artistic legacy. It was only after the Second World War that he became actively involved with the collection, organising numerous exhibitions at home and abroad. During the 1950s he decided that the time had come to secure the collection's future. Encouraged by the Dutch state, which had pledged to build a museum devoted to Van Gogh, he transferred the works he owned to the newly-formed Vincent van Gogh Foundation in 1962. Gerrit Rietveld (1888–1964), an architect of the Stijl movement, produced the first sketches for the museum a year later.

Construction began in 1969; the museum was officially opened on 2 June 1973. The collection, which the Vincent van Gogh Foundation gave on permanent loan to the Dutch state, had found a new home. Over the following decades the museum attracted so many visitors that the decision was taken to expand and thoroughly renovate the building. The new exhibition wing was designed by the Japanese architect Kisho Kurokawa (born 1934) and opened in 1999.

Permanent collection

The museum's permanent collection is on display in the building designed by Gerrit Rietveld. This part of the museum has four floors. The ground and third floor present a broad selection from the museum's holdings of 19th-century European painting and

The Van Gogh museum seen from Museumplein with the new Exhibition Wing at the left

sculpture, supplemented by works by Vincent van Gogh.

The first floor is devoted entirely to Van Gogh's most important works. It contains a large selection of his paintings, which are exhibited in chronological order so that the visitor can follow the development of Van Gogh's oeuvre step by step – from the early works and scenes of peasant life produced in Nuenen, through the artist's experiments with colour and technique in Antwerp and Paris, and culminating in his masterpieces from Arles, Saint-Rémy and Auvers-sur-Oise. Pictures by contemporaries provide the context in which these works were created. Part of the second floor has been designated a study area. Computers, books, educational displays and open storage depots enable visitors to explore the lives and works of 19th-century artists in greater depth. This floor

also accommodates the print room, which is used for regular rotating exhibitions of works on paper from various collections. Van Gogh's drawings and letters are only displayed occasionally, owing to their fragility and sensitivity to light.

Exhibitions

The new wing designed by Kisho Kurokawa is used solely for temporary exhibitions organised by the museum. Ellipse-shaped and partly below ground, the wing's semicircular corridor, two large galleries and print room provide space for exhibitions on various aspects of 19th-century art. The construction of the new wing was financed by a generous donation from The Japan Foundation made possible by funds provided by the Yasuda Fire & Marine Insurance Company, Ltd. of Tokyo, Japan.

The life of Vincent van Gogh

Vincent van Gogh aged 19, early 1873

Vincent van Gogh was born on 30 March 1853 in Zundert, a village in the southern province of Noord-Brabant. He was the eldest son of the Reverend Theodorus van Gogh (1822–1885) and Anna Cornelia Carbentus (1819–1907). The other children in the Van Gogh family were Vincent's sisters Will, Anna and Lies, and his brothers Theo and Cor. Little is known of Vincent's early years other than that he was a quiet child without any obvious artistic talent. The artist would later recall his happy childhood with a great deal of warmth. He received a piecemeal education, attending the village school in Zundert for a year, boarding school in Zevenberg for two years and a state high school in Tilburg for eighteen months.

At the age of 16 he started work at The Hague gallery of the French art dealers, Goupil & Co., a firm in which his uncle Vincent was a partner. Vincent's brother Theo, who was born on 1 May 1857, later worked for the same firm. In August 1872 Vincent and Theo began their exchange of letters which would continue until Vincent's death.

In 1873 Goupil & Co. transferred Van Gogh to London. Two years later the firm moved him to Paris where he lost all ambition to become an art dealer. He immersed himself in religion, threw out his modern, worldly books, and became 'daffy with piety,' in the words of his sister Lies. His work suffered as a result and he was dismissed from Goupil & Co. at the beginning of 1876. Van Gogh then took a job as an assistant teacher in England, but was disappointed by the lack of prospects and returned to Holland at the end of the year. He now decided to follow in his father's footsteps and become a clergyman. Although they were disturbed by his fanaticism and odd behaviour, his parents decided to pay for the private lessons he would need in order to be admitted to university.

However, this proved to be another false start. Van Gogh abandoned the lessons, and went to the Borinage mining region in the south of Belgium, after a brief spell of training as an evangelist. His ministry led him to identify deeply with the miners and their families. However, in 1879 his appointment was not renewed, and his parents despaired, regarding him as a social misfit. In an unguarded moment his father even spoke of committing him to a mental asylum.

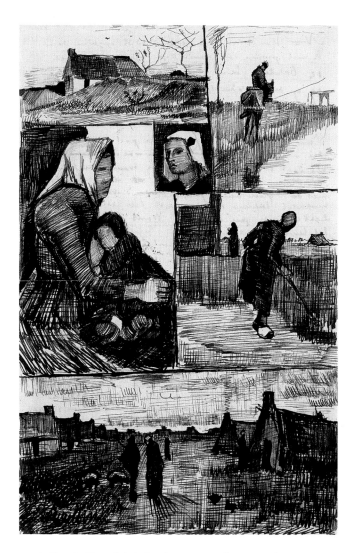

Letters to Theo: left 3 October 1883; right 28 October 1883

A future as an artist

Vincent was also at his wits' end. After a long period of isolation and soul-searching in the Borinage, he decided to follow some advice Theo had given him and become an artist. His earlier desire to serve his fellow men as an evangelist gradually developed into an urge, as he later wrote, to leave mankind 'some memento in the form of drawings or paintings – not made to please any particular movement, but to express a sincere human feeling' [374/309]. Vincent's parents did not approve of this new change of direction and refused to support him. They passed financial responsibility for Vincent to his brother Theo, who was now working in the Paris gallery of art dealers Boussod, Valadon & Cie., the firm which had succeeded Goupil & Co. As a result of Theo's unremitting support Van Gogh later came to regard his oeuvre as the fruit of their joint efforts.

Unsuspected talents

When Van Gogh decided to become an artist, no one, not even Vincent himself, suspected that he possessed extraordinary artistic gifts. He evolved remarkably rapidly from an inept but impassioned novice into a genuine, original master. He proved to have an exceptional flair for bold, harmonious colour effects, and an infallible knack for choosing simple but memorable compositions.

Once Vincent had decided to become an artist he went to Brussels to study at the art academy, but would leave after a few months. It was during this period that he met Anthon van Rappard (1858–1892), who would become his most important artist friend while he remained in the Netherlands.

In April 1881 Van Gogh went to Etten in Noord-Brabant where he moved into his parents' house. Here he endeavoured to master the art of drawing, choosing his subjects mainly from peasant life. He experimented extensively with various materials and concentrated on technical aspects such as perspective, anatomy and physiognomy. At the end of 1881 Van Gogh moved to The Hague where he also focused on drawing. Initially he received lessons in drawing and painting from his cousin-by-marriage Anton Mauve (1838–1888), but the two artists quickly became estranged. One reason for this was that Mauve took exception to Vincent's relationship with Sien Hoornik, a pregnant prostitute who already had a child born out of wedlock.

The vicarage at Nuenen [10]

Although Van Gogh produced several paintings in The Hague, drawing continued to play a greater role in his oeuvre. He drew live models whenever possible, his objective being to become a figure painter. In September 1883 Vincent's relationship with Sien came to an end. Following in the footsteps of other artists such as Van Rappard and Mauve, he went to try his luck in the picturesque heathland of Drenthe, a northern province that was still fairly inaccessible. He left after three months, owing to a lack of materials and models, and moved back in with his parents, who were now living in the village of Nuenen in Noord-Brabant, near Eindhoven.

Nuenen

It was in Nuenen that Van Gogh began to paint with some regularity, modelling himself chiefly on the French painter Jean-François Millet (1814–1875), who had caused a sensation throughout Europe with his scenes of peasant life. Working with iron discipline Van Gogh threw himself into representing the life of peasants and labourers. He also produced many pictures of weavers. In May 1884 he rented rooms from the sexton of the Catholic church, one of which he used as a studio.

In late 1884 Van Gogh started to draw and paint a series of peasants' heads and rough hands. These exercises were a preparation for a large and complex figure painting that the artist hoped to create. In April 1885 they culminated in *The potato eaters*, Van Gogh's masterpiece from his Dutch years.

During the summer of 1885 Van Gogh produced many drawings of the peasants working in the fields. However, he suffered a serious lack of models when the local pastor forbade his parishioners to pose for the artist. So for some time Van Gogh only painted still lifes.

In November 1885, feeling the need for some structured training, Van Gogh went to Antwerp in order to take classes at the academy. Although he was only moderately interested in the tuition, he was highly impressed by the city and its museums. He fell under the spell of Rubens' colouring and brushwork, and first encountered Japanese prints.

Paris

In early 1886 Van Gogh went to live with his brother in Paris. Here he first saw work

View of Paris from Theo's apartment in the rue Lepic [23]

The yellow house in Arles where Van Gogh lived and worked

by the impressionists and post-impressionists, which made the dark palette he had used in The Netherlands seem hopelessly old-fashioned. He began to paint still lifes of flowers, with the aim of mastering a brighter range of colours. In the search for his own idiom, the artist experimented with impressionist and post-impressionist techniques and also studied Japanese prints.

In Paris Van Gogh became friends with other artists such as Paul Gauguin (1848–1903), Emile Bernard (1868–1941), Henri de Toulouse-Lautrec (1864–1901), Paul Signac (1863–1935) and Georges Seurat (1859–1891). Together with Vincent, they would determine the course of modern art. Within two years Van Gogh had become fully acquainted with the latest developments in painting and developed his own, highly personal style.

Arles

In early 1888 Van Gogh went to Arles in southern France where he finally started to have faith in his future as an artist. His ambition was to make a personal contribution to modern art through his daring colour combinations.

The landscape around Arles provided him with a major source of inspiration. In the spring he produced a series of fruit trees in blossom, in the summer a series of golden wheatfields. Although he had some difficulty in recruiting models, he produced a collection of portraits of the Roulin family and various representations of a zouave. He had such faith in his ability that he decided not to sell any work for the time being but to wait until he had assembled thirty high-quality works with which to present himself. Van Gogh hoped that various other artists

would join him in Arles so that they could live and work together. Gauguin's arrival in October 1888 seemed a promising beginning. Towards the end of the year, however, his optimism was rudely shattered by the first signs of his illness, a type of epilepsy accompanied by delusions and psychotic episodes. It was during one of these attacks that he cut off his left earlobe.

Saint-Rémy

In April 1889 Van Gogh went to nearby Saint-Rémy, where he voluntarily committed himself to the Saint-Paul-de-Mausole asylum. Whenever his health permitted he drew or painted in the garden or the countryside around the asylum. The vigorous colours he had used in Arles were now more muted and the brushwork more schematic. During this period Vincent produced a large

Trees and shrubs in the garden of Saint Paul's Hospital in Saint-Rémy, 1889

number of 'translations in colour' of prints by his favourite artists such as Eugène Delacroix (1798–1863) and the already mentioned Jean-François Millet, finding solace in these exercises.

Van Gogh enjoyed a minor success in late 1889 when several of his works were displayed at the fifth exhibition of the Société des artistes indépendants in Paris, and at an exhibition organised by the Belgian avant-garde group of artists Les Vingt. In January 1890 the critic Albert Aurier wrote an article praising Van Gogh's work.

Auvers-sur-Oise

In late May 1890 Van Gogh was discharged from the asylum and moved to the quiet village of Auvers-sur-Oise, north of Paris. En route he stopped in Paris to visit his brother Theo, Theo's wife Johanna van Gogh-Bonger (1862–1925) and their young son Vincent Willem.

Although the artist now had a small but growing circle of admirers, he had lost his original ardour. 'I feel – a failure,' he wrote to his brother. 'That's it as far as I'm concerned – I feel that this is the destiny that I accept, that will never change' [877/648]. Despite this despondency Van Gogh worked hard in Auvers for more than two months, as dozens of drawings and paintings attest. However, life weighed too heavily on him, and on 27 July 1890 he shot himself in the chest, dying two days later. Theo, who had stored the bulk of Vincent's work in Paris, died six months later. Theo's widow returned to Holland with the collection, and dedicated herself to establishing recognition for her late brother-in-law.

In 1914, when Vincent's work now enjoyed widespread admiration, she published the correspondence between the two brothers. From that moment onwards Van Gogh's oeuvre would become inextricably interwoven with the story of his unique and tragic life.

Early work

In December 1881 Van Gogh painted his first pictures under the supervision of his cousin by marriage Anton Mauve (1838–1888). It soon became evident that the novice artist would not be able to produce a confident painting until he had engaged in further study. With this objective in mind he took up drawing again.

Van Gogh made a second attempt to master the art of painting in August 1882. This marine view, painted during the stormy weather which afflicted Scheveningen between 20 and 24 August 1882, is the product of these efforts. 'It blew so hard that I could barely keep standing', Van Gogh wrote [259/226]. While the sand swirled around him he laid out the work using thick daubs of paint and rough brushstrokes. Small grains of sand adhered to the wet paint. Van Gogh had to scrape off the canvas in a small inn behind the dunes and start afresh. The storm had left him with 'a couple of souvenirs' [259/226].

View of the sea at Scheveningen

1   The Hague, August 1882

Oil on canvas, 34.5 x 51 cm

In December 1883 Van Gogh travelled to Nuenen where his father had been pastor since 1882. He moved into the vicarage and stayed there until May 1885, although relations with his parents were strained.

When Van Gogh's mother broke her thighbone in January 1884, this accident brought about a temporary change in their troubled relationship. Vincent and his sister Wil took care of their mother, and any problems faded into the background. Van Gogh painted this view of the Reformed Church in Nuenen as a gift for his mother. Undoubtedly the work was also intended to seal his new relationship with his parents, for the choice of subject indicates that he wished to please his father as well.

In 1885 Van Gogh made several changes to this work, which was probably the first painting he completed in Nuenen. For example, the original figure, a farm labourer, has been replaced by various churchgoers.

Congregation leaving the Reformed Church in Nuenen

2

Nuenen, January-February 1884 and autumn 1885

Oil on canvas, 41.3 x 32.1 cm

The autumn was 'exceptionally lovely' when Van Gogh painted this work in late October 1884 [468/382]. He liked the season so much that he longed for a country 'where it would always be autumn' [277/R15].

Van Gogh wrote to his brother Theo, whom he always kept informed of his progress: 'The latest [work] that I have made is a fairly large study of an avenue of poplars with yellow autumn leaves, in which here and there the sun produces brilliant patches on the fallen leaves on the ground, which are interspersed by the long cast shadows of the tree trunks. At the end of the road [there is] a little cottage and the blue sky above through the autumn leaves' [469/383].

In his letter Van Gogh did not mention the figure that appears in this work. The woman is wearing a mourning hood and cape, and seems to symbolise mourning for she grieves in a landscape which reflects her mood.

Avenue of poplars in autumn

Nuenen, late October 1884
Oil on canvas on panel, 99 x 66 cm

In Nuenen Van Gogh painted many studies of heads. He considered this a vital preparation for figure painting, which he hoped to master at a later date when he attended an academy.

Van Gogh did not regard his studies of heads as portraits of individuals but as depictions of facial types. This is why he sought out 'rough, flat faces with low forehead and thick lips, not that angular [type] but full and Millet-like' [454/372]. The work of French artist Jean-François Millet (1814–1875) and his representations of peasants and peasant life would inspire Van Gogh throughout his artistic career. The woman with the white cap and dark shawl is the Nuenen peasant Gordina de Groot. She can be identified from the *The potato eaters*, for which the De Groot family modelled, as the woman to the left.

Head of a woman

4   Nuenen, March 1885

Oil on canvas, 42.7 x 33.5 cm

Crafts, peasant life

and the village people 'of old Brabant stock' were Van Gogh's favourite subjects during his time in Nuenen [532/423]. In 1884 and 1885 he drew and painted many portraits of Nuenen residents. According to a contemporary he invariably chose the ugliest individuals as his models.

The artist also painted during the evenings in peasants' and labourers' cottages. He was fascinated by the shadows cast by lamplight, and by the effect produced by backlighting. He wrote to Theo: 'I have studies of heads for this, both against the light and with the light, and I have also tackled the entire figure various times, a sewing woman winding thread or peeling potatoes. En face (head on) and en profil (in profile). If I shall ever manage it however I do not know, for it is a difficult effect. Yet I believe I have learned a few things from it' [489/396].

Woman sewing

Nuenen, March-April 1885

Oil on canvas, 43.2 x 34.2 cm

After nearly two years of painting Van Gogh hoped to prove himself to the outside world with his first large figure piece *The potato eaters*. Although the artist realised that his skills were still insufficient for such an ambitious painting with multiple figures, he wished to put his talent to the test. Van Gogh prepared himself thoroughly for this picture, his first masterpiece, painting more than 40 studies of peasants' heads, hands and other elements he planned to include in the composition.

The artist's intention with *The potato eaters* was to produce a naturalistic 'peasant painting' which did not idealise or sentimentalise reality, as he thought other painters did. He wanted to stress the fact that these people 'have dug the earth with the very hands that they are putting in the dish and [...] that they have earned their food so honestly' [501/404]. When painting their faces he aimed for 'the colour of a very dusty potato, unpeeled of course' [502/405].

The potato eaters

Nuenen, mid April-early May 1885

Oil on canvas, 82 x 114 cm

Once *The potato eaters* was finished Van Gogh hoped to produce more 'paintings of a certain stature' [504/407]. Shortly after expressing this wish, he started this picture of a Brabant cottage, which is of a type that had virtually disappeared by this period.

The cottage accommodated two dwellings and had two front doors and a shared chimney. Its occupants – day labourers or weavers – were some of the poorest members of society. Van Gogh, however, was not particularly interested in portraying their poverty for he was fascinated by the symbolism of the old, ramshackle building. 'The subject affected me uncommonly, the two cottages half decayed beneath the same thatched roof reminded me of a couple of old decrepit people who form a single being and whom one sees supporting one other' [509/410].

It also reminded him of a 'wren's nest', which he actually regarded as the loveliest type of bird's nest [510/411].

The cottage

7

Nuenen, mid May 1885

Oil on canvas, 65.7 x 79.3 cm

Together with *The potato eaters* and *The cottage* this painting of the old church tower at Nuenen must be regarded as one of the works in Van Gogh's first series of mature paintings. The artist hoped that this picture would win the recognition of his brother Theo and other Paris art dealers.
The subject of the work is the old church tower and adjacent graveyard in the fields at Nuenen. Although the tower no longer had a function in 1885, the graveyard was still used for burials. The building had been scheduled for demolition for many years, and work had finally started in May. This motivated Van Gogh to record the half-dismantled tower.

The symbolism of the partially demolished church tower inspired Van Gogh to produce an unusual and highly personal interpretation of the structure and its surrounding graveyard. His intention in this painting was to express the idea that although faith and religion perish, the life of the peasant remains unchanged.

The old church tower at Nuenen 'The peasants' churchyard'

8   Nuenen, late May-early June 1885

Oil on canvas, 65 x 80 cm

Van Gogh assembled a variety of objects in his studio, including tools, mosses, plants, hats, caps and stuffed birds. His sister Lies described the room's appearance: 'In a corner of the studio a dead tree was placed, felled during a storm with branch and all, and ever so shrivelled. Somewhat short-ened and set in a pot with earth, this treetop bore an entire collection of bird's nests, gathered by the painter on his rambles through nature'. The children of Nuenen could also earn ten cents by bringing Van Gogh a bird's nest. Specimens from the artist's collection of some thirty different bird's nests formed the subject of five assorted paintings. This painting features five nests, two of which are identical. These two spherical nests, right and centre, were made by wrens who strengthen the nest's entrance with small pieces of straw, as the work clearly shows.

Still life with birds' nests

9

Nuenen, late September-early October 1885 and 1886–87

Oil on canvas, 39.3 x 46.5 cm

This painting represents the vicarage of the Reformed Church at Nuenen where Van Gogh lived with his parents. Following the sudden death of his father on 26 March 1885 Vincent was asked to leave the house by his sister Anna. In late April-early May, he moved into the home of Johannes Schafrat, the Catholic sexton, where he had rented rooms for his studio since May 1884.

Like *Congregation leaving the Reformed Church in Nuenen* this view of the vicarage departs from Van Gogh's usual range of subjects drawn from authentic country life. For this reason it is sometimes assumed that Vincent painted the work as a kind of memento for his brother Theo. Theo had provided his brother with financial aid and moral support from the moment Vincent decided to become an artist. Over the years Theo remained loyal to Vincent and often sent him money or painter's materials.

The vicarage at Nuenen

Nuenen, September-early October 1885

Oil on canvas, 33 x 43 cm

Van Gogh produced this remarkably loosely painted still life in late October 1885, not long after he had practised 'modelling with various colours' [535/424]. He rightly regarded this painting as the climax to his efforts over the previous months.

The still life features a bible alongside a novel by the French writer Emile Zola, *La joie de vivre*. The bible had belonged to Van Gogh's father and probably represents his traditional form of belief. It is open at Isaiah 53, which prophesies the coming of the Redeemer. Vincent himself was fascinated by Zola and French naturalist literature, which he regarded as a kind of bible of modern life. The books appear to symbolise the contrasting views on life held by father and son. The fluent style of painting was inspired by a visit to the Rijksmuseum in Amsterdam, where Van Gogh had been struck by the lively technique employed by Rembrandt van Rijn (1606–1669) and especially Frans Hals (c.1580–1666).

Still life with bible

11

Nuenen, October 1885

Oil on canvas, 65.7 x 78.5 cm

Antwerp and Paris

In late November 1885 Van Gogh moved to the Belgian city of Antwerp. In January 1886 he enrolled at the Royal Academy of Fine Arts where he attended classes in drawing and painting. However, a visit to the museum in Antwerp proved a greater influence on Van Gogh's work than academic tuition. He was impressed by the paintings of the 17th-century master Peter Paul Rubens (1577–1640), about whom he wrote: 'it is very interesting to study Rubens, precisely because he is so outstandingly simple in his technique, or rather seems to be. [He] Does it with so little, and paints and especially draws with such a rapid hand and without any hesitation. But portraits and women's heads or – figures, that is his forte' [555/444]. Inspired by this encounter with Rubens' work Van Gogh produced a fluently painted portrait of a woman with her hair hanging loose. The artist also claimed that the contrast between city women and the peasant women of Nuenen prompted him to develop new ideas, 'particularly concerning the flesh colours' [553/442].

Head of a woman

Antwerp, December 1885

Oil on canvas, 35 x 24 cm

Van Gogh had devised all kinds of plans for earning a living through painting. He thought he could produce city scenes as souvenirs for tourists or paint shop signs. He also hoped that painting portraits would enable him to earn money for what he described as 'greater things' [549/438].

The artist immediately set to work on this portrait project, improving his skills through such exercises as a range of self-portraits. In Paris too, he applied himself to portraiture. This work is one of Van Gogh's earliest attempts to paint himself. It is a study in dark tones which has produced a painting of traditional appearance. Evidently Van Gogh was still struggling with pure portraiture. He would not be able to develop such canvases more fully and endow them with greater vigour until a later stage in his career.

Self-portrait

Paris, autumn 1886

Oil on canvas, 46 x 38 cm

Van Gogh could not bear to stay in Antwerp for long, and moved to Paris in late February 1886. Here he met a number of other artists. His new friends included Henri de Toulouse-Lautrec (1864–1901), Paul Signac (1863–1935), Paul Gauguin (1848–1903) and Emile Bernard (1868–1941), all of whom were to play an important role in the development of modern art. Sketchbook in hand, Van Gogh explored Paris where he drew and painted various views of the city. Initially he continued to paint with dark colours, as he had in Nuenen. This work, for example, still leans heavily on the methods employed by the painters of the Barbizon School. Shortly after its completion, however, Van Gogh would adopt the lighter palette and loose brushstroke of the impressionists. The painting represents a view over Paris to the southeast, with the dome of the Panthéon rising in the centre above a grey sea of houses.

View of Paris

14   Paris, May 1886
Oil on canvas, 54 x 72.5 cm

In the summer of 1886

Van Gogh was inspired by the colourful palette of the impressionists to produce various flower still lifes. He was 'seeking oppositions of blue with orange, red and green, yellow and violet', his aim being to 'harmonise brutal extremes. Trying to render intense colour and not a grey harmony' [572/459a].

Grey harmony can be interpreted as a reference to Van Gogh's earlier work painted in dark colours. In an effort to free himself from these dark tones he painted 'red poppies, blue cornflowers and forget-me-nots, white and pink roses, yellow chrysanthemums' [572/459a]. This flower still life with gladioli was planned as an exercise in richly contrasting, complementary colours.

The influence of the 19th-century painter Adolphe Monticelli (1824–1886) can also be discerned in this picture. The Van Gogh brothers bought paintings by this artist whose works, like *Vase with gladioli and asters*, employ vigorous colour combinations and impasto, or thickly applied paint.

Vase with gladioli and asters

15 Paris, late summer–autumn 1886
Oil on canvas, 46.5 x 38.5 cm

The unusual subject

of this picture, worn-out shoes, provided Van Gogh with the theme for six different paintings. An artist whom Van Gogh had met in Paris later recalled how Vincent had gone in search of the perfect specimens: 'At the flea market he'd bought an old pair of clumsy, bulky shoes – peddler's shoes – but clean and freshly polished. They were fine old clonckers, but unexceptional. He put them on one afternoon when it rained and went for a walk along the old city walls. Spotted with mud, they had become interesting.'

Van Gogh probably saw a deeper meaning in the tattered, old shoes, and may have chosen the subject as a metaphor to represent hard-working labourers and their arduous existence. The painting has occasioned all kinds of psychological speculation, and has been regarded – rightly or wrongly – as a symbol of Van Gogh's troubled path through life.

A pair of shoes

Paris, summer 1886

Oil on canvas, 37.5 x 45 cm

Van Gogh produced his first still lifes in The Hague in 1881, under the supervision of Anton Mauve (1838–1888), one of the masters of The Hague School. Later in his career the artist would continue to realise the benefit of painting various objects in order to master a range of forms and colour nuances. In 1886 Van Gogh produced still lifes of flowers, birds and food. He even used various types of fish as study objects, including bloaters, herring and mackerel. In this small work which features mussels and shrimps the red accents of the shrimps contrast sharply with the blue-black colour of the mussels. Van Gogh sometimes exchanged his paintings for works by another artist. In one instance he was prepared to give away a flower still life in order to acquire two water-colours by the early 19th-century artist Eugène Isabey (1803–1886). He also exchanged a painting of smoked herring for a carpet.

Mussels and shrimps

Paris, autumn 1886

Oil on canvas, 27 x 34 cm

18

The exercises with a lighter palette soon began to pay off, as is evident in this scene set in the café du Tambourin on the boulevard de Clichy. The café du Tambourin can be clearly identified from the interior with its small tables in the shape of a tambourine. Van Gogh regularly came here with his friends from the studio run by Fernand Cormon (1845–1924), where he worked for several months.

The woman with the striking headdress, which is hard to interpret, is probably the café's owner Agostina Segatori from Naples, with whom Van Gogh may have had a brief relationship.

Van Gogh organised an exhibition of Japanese prints at the café which he claimed had a far-reaching influence on the work of his colleagues Emile Bernard and Louis Anquetin (1861–1932). Vague impressions of these prints can be seen on the wall behind Agostina.

Agostina Segatori in the café du Tambourin

Paris, winter 1887–88

Oil on canvas, 55.5 x 46.5 cm

The boulevard de
Clichy in the artists' quarter of
Montmartre lay close to the apartment on the rue Lepic where the
Van Gogh brothers lived. The café
du Tambourin was also in this
neighbourhood, as was Cormon's
studio, while artist friends such as
John Russell (1858–1930), Georges
Seurat (1859–1891) and Paul Signac
(1863–1935) lived close by.
Van Gogh recorded various places
in the district in drawings and
paintings. On the far right of this
work that depicts the boulevard
de Clichy the beginning of the rue
Lepic can be seen, winding up the
hill of Montmartre.

The painting chiefly displays the
influence of impressionism. A fleeting, spontaneously painted impression of 'just a street' was a popular
subject among the artists in this
movement. Van Gogh used a short,
rapid brushstroke to represent the
people, the buildings and the lights
reflecting on the road.

Boulevard de Clichy

Paris, winter 1886–87

Oil on canvas, 46.5 x 55 cm

During Van Gogh's life Montmartre was still somewhat rural in character. However, the picturesque district was being increasingly eaten away by the constantly expanding city.

In this painting Van Gogh concentrated on this distinctively rural area with its mixture of vegetable gardens and farmland. The three windmills were a favourite destination for Parisians on a day out. The largest windmill in the painting, Le Blute-Fin, had a terrace and a lookout point with a fine view over Paris. To the left of the smaller windmill there is evidence of the advancing city: a large apartment block looms over the fields.

The technique employed by Van Gogh in this painting indicates that the artist had become acquainted with neo-impressionism. He used the pointillist method of applying dots in contrasting colours principally for the buildings and vegetable gardens, and painted the sky in a looser, more spontaneous manner.

Vegetable gardens and the Moulin Blute-Fin on Montmartre

20   Paris, spring 1887

Oil on canvas, 44.8 x 81 cm

20

Theo van Gogh kept his mother in Nuenen informed of Vincent's progress as an artist. In 1886 he had written to her that Vincent was mainly painting flowers with the aim of introducing fresher colours into his paintings. These colour studies were not only based on flowers, for simple objects from the artist's surroundings also served as subjects in his still-life paintings. This work from 1887 shows that Van Gogh's studies in colour were helping him develop as an artist. He painted the pot of chives carefully with a fine brush, contrasting many tints of green with red and orange. The decorative wallpaper in the background can also be recognised in other still lifes from the same period, such as *Still life with carafe and lemons*. Van Gogh would increasingly employ a colourful, decorative background in various still lifes and portraits.

Flowerpot with chives

21

Paris, spring-summer 1887
Oil on canvas, 31.5 x 22 cm

During his time in Paris

Van Gogh painted many still lifes which were intended to study the effects of colours in various combinations. For example, he experimented with the complementary contrasts between blue and orange, red and green, and yellow and purple.

Muted colours were gradually replaced by brighter, unmixed tints. Van Gogh used this palette and loose brushstrokes to depict a range of subjects such as books, fruits, plants, crustaceans, and glassware.

This colourful still life has been painted fluently with thin layers of colour; the canvas can be clearly seen through the paint. Van Gogh reproduced the reflections of the light in the water-filled carafe with great virtuosity, and revealed his new mastery of colour theory in a play of complementary colours. The yellow lemons have purple shadows while the green foreground has been set against the red background. Van Gogh was so pleased with the result that he signed the work.

Still life with carafe and lemons

Paris, spring-summer 1887
Oil on canvas, 46.5 x 38.5 cm

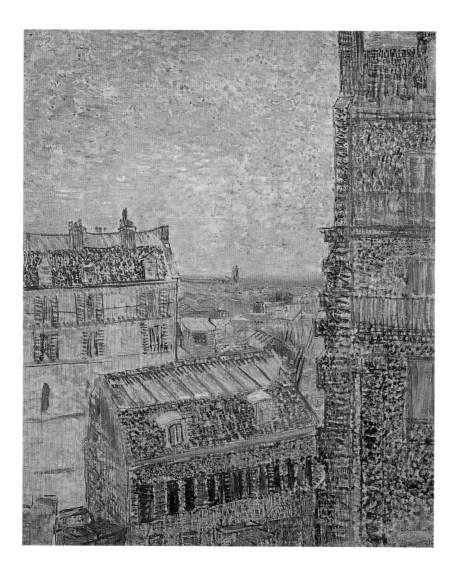

In June 1886 the Van Gogh brothers exchanged the apartment on the rue Laval where they had lived since Vincent's arrival in Paris for a larger dwelling on the rue Lepic.

The brothers were very enthusiastic about the view from their new home. Theo described it thus: 'The most notable feature of our home is that from the windows one has a splendid view over the city with the hills of Meudon, St. Cloud, etc. on the horizon and a piece of sky above as large as when one stands on the dunes. With the various effects produced by variation of the sky, it is a subject for I don't know how many paintings and if you were to see it you would add that it even lends itself to making verses'. Vincent was certainly inspired by the view from the apartment, for he also produced a drawing, an oil sketch and a painting from virtually the same viewpoint.

View of Paris from Theo's apartment in the rue Lepic

23

Paris, spring 1887

Oil on canvas, 46 x 38 cm

Van Gogh had drawn several sketches in the Voyer d'Argenson park in Asnières, a suburb of Paris. This painting, one of the largest he ever produced, is the product of studies that were generally less developed. Van Gogh painted the park in a pointillist manner, a style of painting in which he was highly inter-ested during the summer of 1887. He applied this technique, which juxtaposes small dots of colour, fairly consistently. The painting was carefully composed in the studio and is less spontaneous than many of Van Gogh's other works. The figures in the park are not random passers-by but courting couples whom Van Gogh used to endow the work with a garden of love symbolism.

The painting is the first picture which Van Gogh exhibited in Paris. The fact that the artist considered it suitable for exhibition indicates the importance that he attached to the work.

Courting couples in the Voyer d'Argenson Park in Asnières

Paris, spring 1887
Oil on canvas, 75 x 112.5 cm

This painting was displayed at the exhibition held by a group of young painters, the *Indépendants*, in the spring of 1888. By this time Van Gogh was already living in Arles. Theo sent him Gustave Kahn's review from the *Revue Indépendante* of April 1888. Kahn, a symbolist writer and friend of Seurat and Signac, wrote of the Montmartre landscapes: 'Monsieur van Gogh paints with great vigour and speed [...] large landscapes'. Van Gogh did indeed paint the vegetable gardens on Montmartre with rapid brushstrokes. Although he accurately recorded the layout of this area, his purpose was not precise rendering for his primary intention was to capture the feel of the place.

The canvas is remarkable for its large size. Van Gogh knew that works of this format were hard to sell but he had faith in the painting: 'later people will realise that open air and gaiety reside within it. The whole thing shall then be a decoration for a dining room or country house' [575/462].

Allotments on Montmartre

25

Paris, spring 1887

Oil on canvas, 81 x 100 cm

During the two years Van Gogh spent in Paris, he started a series of self-portraits, producing 35 in total.

The majority of these works can be described as studies, as is certainly the case with this rapidly painted picture. Part of the background has even been left unpainted. The entire work has been painted in mainly yellow tints. Van Gogh only employed a few contours: a black line by the nose and a red line around the neck of his painter's smock.

Van Gogh painted himself several times wearing a straw hat and a painter's smock. He also produced portraits of himself in a smart suit and hat, an ensemble which can be seen in *Self-portrait with felt hat*.

Self-portrait with straw hat and artist's smock

Paris, summer 1887

Oil on card, 40.5 x 32.5 cm

During the summer of 1887 Van Gogh regularly went to the countryside to observe and record nature far from the clamour of the city. These rural subjects were also highly suitable for painting with a colourful palette.

'Isn't yellow lovely' [664/522], Van Gogh later declared in one of his letters, remarking elsewhere: 'No blue without yellow and without orange' [625/B6].
In this painting the artist has opposed the blue of the sky and the yellow of the harvested wheatfield, above and below the yellow-green horizontal band that represents the waving mass of unripe wheat. The only accents are the rising lark and a couple of red poppies between the stalks.

Wheatfield with a lark

27 Paris, June-July 1887

Oil on canvas, 54 x 65.5 cm

During his Dutch period Van Gogh became interested in books which described Japanese prints. He developed an active interest in this form of graphic art in the winter of 1885–1886, while he was in Antwerp where he bought his first Japanese prints. He was particularly taken by the exotic character of these works which he used to decorate his studio. The artist acquired a more serious interest in Paris, when he and his brother Theo assembled a substantial collection of Japanese prints (now in the Van Gogh Museum). It is generally assumed that *The flowering plum tree* is the first of two paintings that Van Gogh based upon a series of woodcuts by the Japanese artist Utagawa Hiroshige (1797–1858). The artist owned twelve examples of Hiroshige's work. For this painting he copied Hiroshige's *The flowering plum tree in the garden of the teahouse in Kameido.*

The flowering plum tree (after Hiroshige)

Paris, summer 1887

Oil on canvas, 55 x 46 cm

'I envy the Japanese for that enormous clarity which all things have to them', Van Gogh wrote in 1888. 'Their work is as easy as breathing and they can make a figure with several well-chosen lines, as if this is as simple as buttoning your jacket' [690/542].

The well-chosen line employed in this painting of a courtesan testifies to Van Gogh's study of Japanese prints. He based this work on a print by the Japanese artist Kesai Eisen (1790–1848), which had appeared on the cover of a themed edition of the magazine *Paris Illustré* in 1886. The artist used a grid to help him copy and enlarge the figure of the Japanese lady. Van Gogh designed a wide border for the picture with waterlilies and bamboo in and around a pool. The cranes and frogs may well allude to the woman's profession for in nineteenth-century Paris 'grue' (crane) and 'grenouille' (frog) were in France common slang terms for prostitutes.

The courtesan (after Eisen)

30   Paris, summer 1887

Oil on canvas, 105.5 x 60.5 cm

In order to become competent in portraiture Van Gogh painted friends, acquaintances and himself. A mirror was an essential aid when painting self-portraits. Van Gogh is known to have purchased a new mirror specifically for self portraiture during his time in Arles. However, the artist produced the majority of his 35 self-portraits, no less than 29, while in Paris.
In this work Van Gogh has depicted himself in a respectable suit and a grey felt hat, a bourgeois counterpart to *Self-portrait with straw hat and artist's smock*. He also experimented with complementary colours and a neo-impressionist technique.
A striking feature of the painting is the halo around the artist's head. This effect did not stem from a desire to present himself as a saint but from his application of the neo-impressionist style. Van Gogh considered this effect so successful that he also used it in other portraits.

Self-portrait with felt hat

31

Paris, winter 1887–88

Oil on canvas, 44 x 37.5 cm

Van Gogh used a special aid, a box with balls of wool, to help him with his colour studies. This box, now in the Van Gogh Museum, contained balls of different coloured wool and various tints of the same colour. The painter would set these balls next to each other or wind threads of different colours together in order to see the effect of various combinations.

Some balls were apparently used for a specific painting: one in particular comprises exactly the same combination of yellows and ochres as in *Still life with quinces and lemons*. The painting may be regarded as a study of various tints of the same colour, in this case yellow, or so-called simultaneous contrast. The work is composed of related tints of ochre, yellow and brown, with the occasional pink, red, green and blue accent. Even the frame has been painted in yellow and ochre. This is the only original painted frame by Van Gogh to have been preserved.

Still life with quinces and lemons

Paris, winter 1887–88

Oil on canvas, 48.5 x 65 cm

In 1881 Van Gogh had painted a still life with cabbages and clogs in a traditional manner using an extremely dark palette. Six years later in Paris he tackled a similar subject. This work clearly shows how far he had progressed in his development as an artist. The dark palette has vanished and been replaced by bright, vigorous colours. The traditional method of representing a still life has been supplanted by a restless dynamic created by Van Gogh's characteristic brushstroke.

Although the striped effect may have been designed to imitate the characteristics of an engraving, it is also possible that Van Gogh used this technique in an effort to breathe new life into the still-life genre.

Still life with cabbages and onions

Paris, winter 1887–88

Oil on canvas, 50 x 64.5 cm

Van Gogh generally used inexpensive materials for his exercises in portraiture. He painted four of his self-portraits over other works, seven on the back of studies from his Nuenen period and a further seven on card, which was much cheaper than linen canvas. He wrote to Theo concerning such experiments: 'if I manage to paint the colours of my own face, something which is not without its problems, I can also paint the heads of other men and women' [685/537]. In this self-portrait painted on card the artist has chosen to immortalise himself in a respectable suit. It is loosely painted, the colour and treatment being based upon pointillist theories. However, Van Gogh has painted the face in a more traditional manner, incorporating greater detail than in the clothing.

Self-portrait

34   Paris, spring 1887

Oil on card, 41 x 33 cm

From an early age Van Gogh had been considerably influenced by books, and his letters contain regular references to contemporary literature. This work depicts nearly two dozen books, mostly with yellow covers, lying open or stacked in small piles. The yellow covers indicate that these are modern French novels, which were published at that period in this form.

This lavish assembly of naturalistic novels may be regarded as Van Gogh's homage to this specific style of literature. The artist's letters to his sister Wil in particular show that Van Gogh found the same solace in reading these novels as he had once derived from the bible. This work is a study for a slightly larger painting exhibited in 1888. Unlike some of his other still lifes of books, Van Gogh has not endeavoured to make the titles legible.

Study for 'Romans Parisiens'

Paris, winter 1887–88
Oil on canvas, 53 x 73.2 cm

In February 1887 Theo wrote to his mother that Vincent was working on improving his portrait painting skills. He informed her that his brother had painted various successful portraits, although he had not been paid for these.

Van Gogh carefully created this work with fine brushstrokes in subtle colours. He painted the background and the man's clothes in muted tints, while he composed the face of small stripes in a range of colours.

The identity of the man in the portrait cannot be established with any certainty. However, he could be Lucien Martin, who owned a restaurant on the avenue de Clichy. Van Gogh organised an exhibition of work by himself and by his friends in this restaurant. His art was exhibited on several occasions in Paris, in various cafés, restaurants and art dealer's galleries. However, none was sold.

Portrait of a restaurant owner, possibly Lucien Martin

Paris, winter 1886–87
Oil on canvas, 65.5 x 54.5 cm

In his many self-portraits Van Gogh generally concentrated on representing his head and facial expression. This *Self-portrait as an artist* is one of the few works in which he included more of his body. The artist has posed himself at an easel, holding a palette and brushes. He has employed a looser brushstroke which displays his mastery of the neo-impressionist technique.

The painting reflects Van Gogh's state of mind during his final months in Paris. He described the work to his sister Wil: 'A pink-grey countenance with green eyes, ashen hair, lines on the forehead and around the mouth, stiff, wooden, an extremely red beard, quite desperate and sad' [633/W4]. He would leave Paris in February 1888 and travel to southern France in good spirits in search of new, inspiring surroundings.

Self-portrait as an artist

37 Paris, February 1888
Oil on canvas, 65.5 x 50.5 cm

In February 1888 Van

Gogh went to southern France. There he hoped to find a little of the ambiance which he so admired in Japanese prints. During the journey he saw snow-covered countryside and immediately compared this to the winter landscapes produced by Japanese artists.

When Van Gogh arrived in Arles he was surprised by the coldest February for 28 years, with a blanket of snow lying some 60 centimetres thick. He painted the wintry landscape on a couple of occasions but the cold forced him to work indoors.

However bleak the weather was outside, inside Van Gogh had a hopeful sign that spring was on the way. Around 3 March he wrote: 'It is freezing considerably here and there is still snow on the ground, I have a study of a white landscape with the town in the background. Also 2 small studies of an almond sprig which is already in blossom nevertheless' [584/466].

Sprig of flowering almond blossom in a glass

38   Arles, March 1888

Oil on canvas, 24 x 19 cm

A month after arriving in southern France Van Gogh painted the drawbridge over the canal at Arles. The bridge was officially called the 'Pont de Réginelle' but was known as the Pont de Langlois (Langlois Bridge), after its bridge keeper.

Van Gogh produced various versions of the subject, as was his custom. The work in the Van Gogh Museum is the last of a series of three, and also the simplest. Van Gogh's intention with this painting was to depict a Provençal landscape which he thought exuded a Dutch ambience, or, as he himself put it: 'something comical [...] such as I shall not make every day' [594/473]. Unlike the rapidly painted grass and foreground path, the bridge has been depicted in great detail. Van Gogh has successfully rendered the various materials from which the bridge was constructed: the stone parapet, the thick wooden beams and even the ropes used to raise the bridge, although the original red of these has faded.

The Langlois bridge

Arles, March 1888
Oil on canvas, 59.5 x 74 cm

The bustling city of Paris had exhausted Van Gogh physically and mentally. In a letter to his sister Wil he explained his reason for moving to Arles: 'I have perceived too much that in the winter I can make headway neither with my work, nor with my health' [582/W2].

When spring arrived in Arles the artist was certainly able to make progress with his work. Nature in southern France inspired him to produce a large number of landscapes. Between 24 March and 21 April 1888 Van Gogh painted fourteen canvases with blossoming fruit trees. He hoped that the subjects – 'motifs […] which give everyone pleasure' – would sell well [595/475].

While he was painting these canvases Van Gogh developed the idea of grouping the works in decorative ensembles. The Van Gogh Museum owns three paintings of orchards in blossom that which were originally intended to form part of such a group. This particular painting of a pear tree in full blossom, with an almost invisible butterfly at its centre, was once the central work in an orchard triptych.

Small pear tree in blossom

Arles, April 1888

Oil on canvas, 73 x 46 cm

'I am working as one possessed', Vincent wrote in April 1888. 'For the trees are in blossom and I would like to produce a Provençal orchard of incredible gaiety' [594/473]. He urged Theo to send him new paint: 'In God's name send me that paint at once. The season of blossoming orchards is just so short' [595/475].

Van Gogh worked on tirelessly, despite a strong wind – as he himself wrote – which made it hard for him to work on three out of four days. However, the artist fastened his easel to pegs which he sunk in the ground, allowing him to continue painting outdoors. During one of these sessions in late March 1888 he painted an orchard in blossom, a work with which he was extremely satisfied. He sent it as a tribute to the widow of the painter Mauve who had recently died. Shortly afterwards he painted a second, slightly larger version of the subject. This is the canvas now in the Van Gogh Museum.

The pink peach tree

41

Arles, April 1888

Oil on canvas, 80.5 x 59 cm

After working single-mindedly on various orchard paintings in the spring of 1888, Van Gogh focused his attention during the summer almost entirely on wheatfields and the harvest. In June 1888 the artist produced ten paintings and five drawings of such subjects in just over a week. He worked in the fields every day, beneath the scorching sun, until a violent storm on 20 June brought an unexpected end to harvest time.

The waving wheat offered Van Gogh an opportunity to experiment with brushstroke and colour. In this painting he has set the golden yellow of the ripe wheat against a colourful swirl of yellow, green, red, brown and black in the foreground. The horizon is extremely high, so virtually the entire painting is covered with the colours of the crops in the fields.

Wheatfield

42   Arles, June 1888

Oil on canvas on card, 54 x 65 cm

In Arles Van Gogh thought that he recognised something of the character that so fascinated him in Japanese prints. He wrote to his sister Wil: 'I always pretend that I am in Japan here; and that consequently I only have to keep my eyes open and only have to paint what impresses me in my immediate surroundings' [681/W7].

These surroundings included the orchards and wheatfields which Van Gogh painted in series. He also saw Japan in this field with flowers near Arles. 'A meadow full of brightly coloured yellow buttercups, a ditch full of irises with green leaves and purple flowers'; their contrasting colours inspired the artist. Van Gogh concluded: 'A little town surrounded by a field full of yellow and purple flowers; you know, that is precisely a Japanese dream' [611/487].

Field with flowers near Arles

43   Arles, May 1888

Oil on canvas, 54 x 65 cm

While in Nuenen Van Gogh had already written that summer, unlike spring, was not so easy to depict. He intended to capture the mood of a summer's day through 'an opposition of blues against an element of orange in the golden bronze of the wheat' [454/372]. In this painting the artist has successfully depicted such a 'summer sun effect'. However, Van Gogh was not simply interested in portraying a sunny landscape. His primary intention was to reflect rural life, and the painting also depicts the various stages of harvest. Although the peasant's activities are presented at a distance, Van Gogh considered these an essential part of the painting which he even entitled *La moisson*, or 'harvest'. The artist regarded this work as one of his most successful paintings. 'The [...] canvas thoroughly beats all the others', he declared three times in a letter to his brother Theo from Arles [627/497].

The harvest

Arles, June 1888

Oil on canvas, 73 x 92 cm

In late May 1888 Van Gogh decided to paint seascapes around the Mediterranean coast. He thought of going to Marseilles or Martigues, but finally headed for the little old fishing town of Les Saintes-Maries-de-la-Mer. Although Van Gogh only stayed there for a few days, he managed to complete nine drawings, two seascapes and a view of the town. As he was leaving Saintes-Maries he made a drawing of the boats: 'That was before the boats put out to sea posthaste, I had observed it every morning, but because they left very early, I had no time to paint it' [623/487].

Back in his studio in Arles Van Gogh had plenty of time to create a painting based on his sketches. In a letter to Bernard he described this studio work as a composition of 'small green, red and blue boats, so lovely in respect of form and colour that they recall flowers' [625/B6].

Fishing boats on the beach at Les Saintes-Maries-de-la Mer
Arles, June 1888
Oil on canvas, 65 x 81.5 cm

Van Gogh immortalised in Les Saintes-Maries-de-la-Mer such subjects as the old town, fishing boats on the beach and the sea. This work portrays the effects of light on the water, with small boats returning from fishing. Back in Arles Vincent described how fascinated he had been by the Mediterranean. He thought that its waters had a 'a colour like that of mackerel, that is to say variable – you do not ever know if it is green or purple, you do not ever know if it is blue, because the next moment the ever-changing lustre has taken on a pink or grey tint' [622/499]. This 'mackerel colour' is a central feature of the canvas. The artist has alternated blue and green brush-strokes to suggest the varying tints in the water. Van Gogh set his signature lower left in a conspicuous bright red, his motive being to introduce 'a red note in the green' [665/524].

Seascape near Les Saintes-Maries-de-la-Mer

Arles, June 1888

Oil on canvas, 51 x 64 cm

Van Gogh's dream was to found a colony of artists where like-minded individuals could live and work together. He thought that a collective studio could be established in the rooms that he rented in May 1888 in the right section of the yellow house on place Lamartine in Arles. Vincent had the apartment redecorated: 'I want to make a true artists' house of it, but not expensive, on the contrary, nothing expensive, but everything – from the chair to the painting – with character' [680/534].

In his studio he painted *The yellow house*, a description of which he sent to his brother Theo: 'For it is tremendous, those yellow houses in the sun and then the incomparable clarity of the blue. [...] The house to the left is pink with green shutters, that stands in the shadow of a tree, that is the restaurant where I go to eat every day. My friend, the postman, lives at the end of the street to the left, between two railway bridges' [695/543].

The yellow house 'The street'

47

Arles, September 1888

Oil on canvas, 72 x 91.5 cm

Van Gogh's bedroom

was furnished with simple pinewood furniture and his own paintings. Above his bed he hung his portraits of the Belgian poet Eugène Boch and the soldier Paul-Eugène Milliet.

Van Gogh used bright, contrasting planes of colour to depict his bedroom. The work is characterised by thickly applied paint and a curious three-dimensional effect. The rear wall of the room appears to stand at a strange angle to the other walls, although this is not a mistake but an observation by the painter based on fact. In other places, however, objects seem to stand or lie at unnatural angles as Van Gogh did not strictly apply the rules of per-spective. He had a reason for this, which he explained in a letter to his brother Theo: he had con-sciously painted the interior 'flat' and excluded all shadows in order to make the work resemble a Japanese print. The simple interior and clear colours were intended to express 'rest' or 'sleep' literally and figuratively.

The bedroom

Arles, October 1888
Oil on canvas, 72 x 90 cm

According to Van Gogh *The zouave* was 'a boy with a small face, a bull neck, a tiger's glance' [631/501]. The subject of this portrait is dressed in the uniform of the zouaves, a French infantry regiment. 'It is harsh and all in all ugly and failed', Van Gogh wrote to Bernard concerning this portrait. But he continued: 'Yet it is all right, as I have tackled real difficulties with it, preparing the way for the future' [635/B8].

The artist was referring here to his efforts to reconcile the colours of the uniform and the background. Van Gogh continued: 'It is thus a raw combination of colours that do not match, not easy to execute – the studies I have made of it, I consider terribly harsh and yet I would always like to work on portraits of the common people, even garish portraits such as this. I learn from these and that is what I chiefly crave from my work' [631/501].

49

The zouave

Arles, June 1888

Oil on canvas, 65 x 54 cm

During the initial weeks of autumn 1888 Van Gogh worked with great enthusiasm on a new series of rustic scenes. From time to time he was hampered by rainy weather: 'This was a little inconvenient, but in the sunny periods in between I have just completed a canvas [...] on which ploughed fields are depicted. A blue sky with white clouds, an immense piece of land of ash-coloured lilac, countless furrows and clods of earth, the horizon of blue hills and green bushes with small farms with orange roofs' [691/541a].

This work was described by Van Gogh as 'clods of earth mellow in colour [...] like a pair of clogs [...] with a sky of forget-me-not blue, fluffs of white clouds' [692/541].

The canvas is painted with thick brushstrokes. Vincent warned his brother Theo that it should dry for a long time, for 'with paintings with thick impastos you should proceed as with strong wine – it has to lie' [691/541a].

Ploughed fields 'The furrows'

Arles, September 1888
Oil on canvas, 72.5 x 92.5 cm

Gauguin came to Arles in late October. Van Gogh was delighted by the arrival of his colleague which he regarded as marking the start of his 'atelier du Midi'. For two months the artists shared the yellow house and worked together.

Van Gogh created this painting in November 1888. The motif of an empty chair has often served as a personification of its owner. This was certainly Van Gogh's intention when he painted the canvas, which is really a portrait of his friend Gauguin.

During the same period Van Gogh also produced a painting of his own, plainer chair (London, National Gallery). This work may be regarded as the pendant to *Gauguin's chair*. In these two paintings Van Gogh may have intended to symbolically represent the friends' contrasting characters. Unfortunately it was these differences in personality which caused the relationship between the two artists to deteriorate.

Gauguin's chair

51

Arles, November 1888

Oil on canvas, 90.5 x 72.5 cm

'There is no better

and quicker way to improve work
than by painting figures' [658/517],
Van Gogh wrote during his time in
Arles. So he confidently started a
series of portraits of the Roulin
family.

Van Gogh had made friends with
the postman Joseph Roulin, who
lived not far from the yellow house.
In December 1888 he decided to
immortalise Roulin's entire family.
He wrote to his brother Theo that
he had made portraits 'of an entire
family, that of the postman, of
whom I have earlier done the head:
husband, wife, baby, the little boy
and the 16-year-old son, all types
and truly French, although they
look like Russians' [728/560].
He produced more than twenty
works, including this portrait of a
shy-looking boy. It is 'the little boy'
mentioned in the letter, Joseph
Roulin's eleven-year-old son,
Camille.

Portrait of Camille Roulin

52 Arles, December 1888

Oil on canvas, 40.5 x 32.5 cm

Van Gogh was fascinated by the theme of the sower. As early as 1880 he had made a copy of *The sower* by Millet, his great hero when depicting peasant life. Later, in Arles, Van Gogh produced his own variations on this theme. A striking feature of this work is the setting sun which frames the sower's head like a halo. In a letter to the artist Emile Bernard Van Gogh described the sower and the wheatsheaf as symbols of infinity, thereby alluding to the cycle of growth, blossoming and harvest that is heralded by the act of sowing. At a later date he would work on the motif of the reaper, in which he saw the image of death: 'in the sense that mankind represents the corn which is being reaped. If you like it is thus the opposite of the sower which I have previously attempted' [801/604]. The sower therefore symbolises life and vitality.

The sower

Arles, November 1888
Oil on canvas, 32 x 40 cm

The tensions between Van Gogh and Gauguin gradually escalated, and the situation deteriorated until 23 December 1888 when Van Gogh cut off part of his left ear in a fit of madness. Gauguin fled to Paris and Van Gogh was admitted to the hospital in Arles. During his enforced stay in the hospital Van Gogh remembered the blossoming orchards which he had painted in the spring of 1888. He was afraid that his committal would cause him to miss the beginning of the blossom season. However, he was released from the hospital in early April and immediately embarked on a new series of orchard canvases.

Van Gogh described this work to Signac as 'almost entirely green with a little lilac and grey – on a rainy day' [760/583b]. He attempted to paint the falling rain with several long brushstrokes in the grass.

Orchards in blossom, view of Arles

54   Arles, April 1889

Oil on canvas, 50.5 x 65 cm

A symphony in blue and yellow was how Van Gogh thought the interior of the yellow house should appear when Gauguin arrived. He wanted to impress his friend with a series of decorative still lifes of sunflowers. These still lifes were to grace the walls of Gauguin's bedroom and be framed with 'thin slats of wood, painted in red lead' [669/B15].

Van Gogh started the series with great ardour. He had to work quickly as the flowers quickly wilted in a vase: 'I am painting with the enthusiasm of a resident of Marseilles eating bouillabaisse [Provençal fish soup], which shall not surprise you, when it involves painting large sunflowers' [670/526].

Gauguin considered the paintings highly successful and declared that sunflowers should be Van Gogh's trademark. In 1889 Van Gogh tackled the motif once more, in this canvas now in the Van Gogh Museum.

Sunflowers

Arles, January 1889

Oil on canvas, 95 x 73 cm

Saint-Rémy

After his release from the hospital in Arles, Van Gogh continued to be troubled by epileptic fits. So in May 1889 he had himself voluntarily committed to an asylum for the mentally ill in nearby Saint-Rémy.

The physician who attended Van Gogh, doctor Peyron, allowed the artist to continue painting. Theo rented an extra room in the asylum for his brother to use as a studio. In the garden of the asylum Van Gogh saw this moth which he mistakenly described as a death's-head moth (it is actually an emperor moth): 'Yesterday I drew a large, quite rare moth which is called a death's-head moth, with marvellously fine colours, black, grey, off-white with a red lustre (though it inclines slightly to olive-green); it is very large. In order to paint it I had to kill it and that was a pity, so lovely was the creature' [778/592]. So Van Gogh based this little painting of a moth against a background of arums on a detailed drawing.

Emperor moth

Saint-Rémy, May 1889

Oil on canvas, 33.5 x 24.5 cm

This Pietà – a representation of Mary grieving over the body of Christ – is based on a lithograph after a painting by Eugène Delacroix (1798–1863). The incentive for Van Gogh to produce this work was an accident: 'that lithograph by Delacroix, la pietà, fell in the oil and paint with some other prints and was damaged. I was distressed by this – in the meantime I have been engaged in painting [a copy after] it and you will see it one day' [802/605]. The lithograph – complete with stain – has also been preserved.

Religious works such as the *Pietà* are an exception in the painter's oeuvre. It is not implausible that sick and 'misunderstood' Van Gogh identified with Christ in His suffering. He wrote: 'I am not indifferent and in suffering itself religious thoughts sometimes give me a great deal of comfort' [802/605]. Some critics stress the painter's resemblance to the red-bearded Christ figure in the *Pietà*.

Pietà (after Delacroix)
Saint-Rémy, September 1889
Oil on canvas, 73 x 60.5 cm

Van Gogh had no difficulty finding subjects in Saint-Rémy: he worked in the asylum's garden, drew the corridors of the building and the barred windows, painted the view and made portraits of several patients. Occasionally he was also allowed to work outside the asylum – under supervision. In *Wheatfield with a reaper* the artist depicted the view from the window of his room: a hedged wheatfield with mountains in the background. The corn is represented with long, undulating brushstrokes, which occasionally form spirals. Van Gogh would later describe the painting's meaning, with reference to a well-known biblical image: 'In that reaper – a vague shape who battles like a devil in the intense heat to finish his work – I saw the image of death, in the sense that the corn represents mankind being reaped' [801/604]. He did add, however, that it was a death figure 'almost with a smile' [801/604].

Wheatfield with a reaper

Saint-Rémy, September 1889
Oil on canvas, 74 x 92 cm

In Saint-Rémy Van Gogh made a series of paintings after prints by artists such as Honoré Daumier (1808–1879), Rembrandt van Rijn (1606–1669) and especially Jean-François Millet (1814–1875), who had also provided him with regular inspiration during his early career. He continued to produce such works, even when mental crises prevented him from going outside the asylum to paint.

He wrote to Theo concerning copying: 'I started on it by chance and I think that I learn from it and that above all it sometimes offers solace too. Then my brush moves between my fingers like a bow on a violin and entirely for my pleasure' [806/607].

Van Gogh copied the *Travaux des champs* series by Millet in ten small pictures, seven of which are now in the Van Gogh Museum. These are mainly painted in golden yellow and clear blue, the colours that Van Gogh chiefly associated with peasant life.

Peasant woman binding sheaves (after Millet)

Saint-Rémy, September 1889
Oil on canvas, 43 x 33 cm

During the year Van Gogh spent in the asylum he painted a nearby quarry on two occasions. While engaged on one version of this subject, he suffered a fit that made it impossible for him to work in the months that followed.

Despite this setback Van Gogh wanted to send the canvas, which he later finished, to his brother Theo, describing it as 'an experiment that was soberer, muted and discreet in colour, mixed greens, reds and rusty ochre yellows' [798/601]. A month later he did indeed send the work to his brother. The letter accompanying the package indicates that the artist was satisfied with his painting: 'I think the Entrance to a quarry, which I was doing when I felt the fit coming, is fairly good, because to my taste the dark greens go well with the ochre tints. There is something sad in it which is healthy and that is why I like it' [806/607].

Entrance to a quarry

Saint-Rémy, July 1889

Oil on canvas, 60 x 74.5 cm

Van Gogh had already derived a great deal of inspiration from the extensive gardens around the asylum. When autumn came, a season for which the artist had a marked preference, he produced various studies of autumn effects in the nearby park.

Van Gogh chose a high viewpoint for this autumn scene. As a result the tree trunk silhouettes have been cropped by the upper and lower edges of the painting. Van Gogh knew this compositional form from works by Emile Bernard and Gauguin. It is a genuine study, in which parts of the canvas have been left unpainted.

Vincent wrote to Theo that when the leaves started to fall southern landscapes increasingly reminded him of northern (i.e. Dutch) land-scapes. During his illness Van Gogh reminisced a great deal about his youth and early adulthood in the Netherlands.

The garden of Saint-Paul's Hospital 'The fall of the leaves'

63 Saint-Rémy, October 1889

Oil on canvas, 73.5 x 60.5 cm

After suffering an epileptic fit in July 1889 Van Gogh did not venture outdoors for two months, fearing another sudden attack. He did not summon up the courage to work outside again until October. By early November he had finished 'an evening effect with large pine trees' [818/613]. 'You should understand', Van Gogh wrote, summarising the canvas' effect for his artist friend Bernard, 'that the combination of red ochre, green that has been made darker with grey and the black stripes which indicate the contours, induce the feeling of terror from which some of my companions in adversity sometimes suffer, so-called "black-red"'[824/B21].

Van Gogh often painted a second version, of his subject. He created this repetition of the asylum garden, now in the Van Gogh Museum, in his studio. This probably explains why the work has been composed more carefully and employs a more systematic use of colour and brushstroke than the first version which the artist painted in situ.

The garden of Saint-Paul's Hospital

Saint-Rémy, November 1889
Oil on canvas, 71.5 x 90.5 cm

In January 1890 Theo wrote to Vincent that his wife Johanna had given birth to a son. The baby was to be named Vincent Willem, after his godfather. As a gift for the new arrival Vincent painted a picture of one of his favourite subjects, large branches of blossom against a blue sky. He thought that the work could be hung above Theo's marital bed. Vincent chose the branches of the almond tree as a symbol of young life for the almond is one of the earliest trees to blossom, heralding spring in February. The artist drew his inspiration for the well-defined contouring and positioning of the tree in the picture plane from Japanese prints. Over the years the painting has lost some of its colour. The blossom which now appears to be predominantly white was originally more pink.

Almond blossom

Saint-Rémy, February 1890

Oil on canvas, 73.5 x 92 cm

Van Gogh derived the subject of this work, a snowy field with agricultural implements and crows flying, from a print, an etching by Alfred Delauney (1876–1941) after a painting by Millet. Van Gogh borrowed the composition of the black-and-white print and added colour, in his own characteristic brushstroke. He made the landscape even more wintry and desolate than in Millet's painting, although this bleakness has also been unintentionally exaggerated by the fact that the painting's original purple hue has faded to blue-green. The work is Van Gogh's own variation on Millet's theme rather than a true copy of the original. Concerning copying Van Gogh wrote: 'especially now I am ill, I am trying to produce something to comfort me, something for my own pleasure: I set down the black-and-white image of a print after either Delacroix or Millet as a subject for me. And then I improvise on this with colour' [806/607].

Snow-covered field with a harrow (after Millet)

66 Saint-Rémy, January 1890
Oil on canvas, 72 x 92 cm

After staying only three days in Paris, in May 1890, Vincent left the bustling, restless city for the rural quiet of Auvers-sur-Oise. One of the residents of this village, thirty kilometres to the northwest of Paris, was doctor Paul Gachet. A physician and amateur painter Gachet had been a friend of Monticelli and had assembled an

art collection that included works by Paul Cézanne (1839–1906), Auguste Renoir (1841–1919) and Camille Pissarro (1830–1903). It was Pissarro who had suggested that Theo should contact Gachet and ask him if he could take Vincent under his wing. Gachet did indeed keep an eye on Van Gogh who he encouraged in his

work. Three weeks after arriving in Auvers Van Gogh wrote that he had found a true friend in Gachet. The artist liked Auvers, where he felt 'a tranquillity à la Puvis de Chavannes' [879/637]. This gave him the sense of calm which he needed to produce many works in a short time, such as this landscape.

View of Auvers

69 Auvers-sur-Oise, May 1890

Oil on canvas, 50 x 52 cm

Auvers was a real artists' village where painters such as Armand Guillaumin (1841–1927), Camille Pissarro (1830–1903) and Paul Cézanne (1839–1906) had worked. Charles-François Daubigny (1817–1878), an artist whose work Van Gogh much admired, had also lived there.

Daubigny belonged to an earlier generation than Van Gogh. A popular landscape painter of the Barbizon School, he had produced many of his paintings in situ, in the open air.

When Van Gogh moved to Auvers, Daubigny's widow was still living in the village. There was a large garden attached to Daubigny's house which Van Gogh painted several times. This impressionist-style work depicts part of the garden, and is probably a study for two larger paintings that show the entire plot.

Daubigny's garden

Auvers-sur-Oise, June 1890

Oil on canvas, 50.7 x 50.7 cm

Vincent wrote to his brother Theo: 'Auvers is very beautiful'. There were 'many old thatched roofs, something that is becoming rare [...] it is entirely rural, distinct and picturesque' [874/635]. The fields and countryside around Auvers also became the subject of his paintings. He described this study in a letter to Gauguin, with whom he remained in contact despite the incident in Arles: 'nothing but ears of wheat, blue-green stalks, long leaves like ribbons, green & pink through the reflected light; slightly yellowed ears with a pale pink edge produced by the dusty type of flower, at the bottom a pink convolvulus winds around a stem' [893/643]. Van Gogh later used this close-up of wheat as the decorative motif in the background to a portrait. He intended the effect produced by the colours to evoke 'the gentle rustling of the ears of wheat which sway to and fro in the wind' [893/643].

Ears of wheat

71

Auvers-sur-Oise, June 1890

Oil on canvas, 64.5 x 47 cm

In early July 1890 Van
Gogh briefly visited his brother in
Paris. There he met the French art
critic Albert Aurier, who had written
an enthusiastic article in January
1890 about the works which Van
Gogh had submitted to an exhibition
in Brussels. Van Gogh's submission
to the *Salon des Indépendants* in
Paris that same year had also met

with a positive response. Despite
this growing appreciation for his
work, however, Van Gogh felt he
had failed as an artist.
He hastily returned to Auvers
where he produced this work in
twilight mood. He painted the landscape shortly after sunset, in the
vicinity of the chateau. The artist
described it as: 'An evening effect:

two pear trees entirely black
against the yellowing sky, with
wheatfields and the chateau
enclosed by dark foliage against
the purple background' [896/644].
During his time in Auvers Van Gogh
produced various works in this
striking format, whose width is
twice its height, making it highly
suitable for substantial landscapes.

Landscape at twilight

Auvers-sur-Oise, June 1890

Oil on canvas, 50 x 101 cm

In Auvers Vincent painted a number of landscapes with wheatfields in an unusual, elongated format (50 x 100 cm). He wrote about these canvases in a letter to his brother Theo: 'They are enormous sweeping wheatfields beneath stormy skies and I have intentionally tried to express sadness, extreme loneliness in them'

[903/649]. The simple composition of *Wheatfield under thunderclouds* – a division into two horizontal planes – emphasises the boundless quality of the open fields. There is no tree, bird or figure to interrupt the horizontal character of the landscape.

However, the painter claimed that these works also contained a posi-

tive meaning: 'I am almost sure that in these canvases I have articulated what I cannot express in words, namely how healthy and heartening I find the countryside' [903/649]. Van Gogh intended to take these elongated canvases to Paris in the near future, but this was not to be.

Wheatfield under thunderclouds

Auvers-sur-Oise, July 1890

Oil on canvas, 50 x 100.5 cm

Two paintings contends for the dubious honour of being Van Gogh's final work: *Tree-roots* and *Wheatfield with crows*. However, this contest will never be decided for the only certainty is that Vincent also produced this painting during the last weeks of his life. In 1882 Van Gogh had already made several drawings of tree roots whose intended message he described as follows: 'compulsive and passionate rooting in the earth and yet being half torn loose by storms. I wanted to express something of the life struggle in those black, knobbly roots with their gnarls' [221/195]. It is tempting to see the same symbolism in this painting of grotesque tree roots produced eight years later. The almost abstract shapes of the roots could represent Van Gogh's life struggle and the impending uprooting of his existence. However, it is not known if Van Gogh actually intended the work to contain this message.

Tree-roots

Auvers-sur-Oise, July 1890
Oil on canvas, 50 x 100 cm

During the final weeks of his life Van Gogh was quite depressed. He was worried about his own financial situation and that of his brother Theo, who was having problems with his employers, the art dealers Boussod, V~~~~~n & Cie. Vinc~~~~~~~~~~~~~ as a burden ~~~~~~ Theo's young family.

Vincent painted *Wheatfield with crows* during these weeks, and the work is sometimes interpreted as an omen of Van Gogh's imminent suicide. However, this theory is probably incorrect as the subject is traditional and can be found in works by painters of the Barbizon School. Moreover, in his final letter

to Theo, dated 23 July, Vincent ordered new paint, suggesting that he still had many plans for new paintings, although he would never execute these. On 27 July the artist shot himself in the chest. He died of his wounds two days later, with his brother at his side.

Wheatfield with crows

Auvers-sur-Oise, July 1890

Oil on canvas, 50.5 x 103 cm

The colourist

Jules Dupré worked around Barbizon together with such painters as Théodore Rousseau (1812–1867) and Constant Troyon (1810–1865). Dupré painted *The sunken path* in the period 1835–1840.

A striking feature of this work is the contrast between the clear blue sky and the dark trees and areas of shadow to the right and in the foreground. This effect is further reinforced by the use of expressive, clearly visible brushstrokes for the landscape and a fine, smooth finish for the sky. The artist has represented a herd of cows with a few effective dabs of paint. These animals are missing in a second version of the painting, now in a private collection, which Dupré produced during the same period.

Van Gogh was charmed by Dupré's use of colour in which he discerned 'a trace of a magnificent symphony. That symphony is amazingly calculated and yet simple and infinitely deep as nature itself' [453/371].

Jules Dupré 1811–1889
The sunken path, c. 1835–1840
Oil on canvas, 101 x 83 cm

During the summer

Corot and Théodore Rousseau (1812–1867) would base themselves in the village of Barbizon, near Paris, from where they would paint the surrounding landscape. Other artists sometimes joined them, forming a group that became known as the Barbizon School.

Until this time artists had generally used landscape as a background for classical, historical or biblical scenes. The Barbizon painters elevated nature to a subject in its own right. Their freer style of painting, lighter palette and interest in light effects make them the forerunners of the impressionists.

Van Gogh greatly admired the use of colour and striking light effects in paintings by 'Father Corot', as he called the French artist in his letters. He declared that he was spellbound by the peace and serenity that radiated from Corot's work.

Jean Baptiste Camille Corot 1796–1875
Souvenir of 'Les Landes', c. 1850–1860
Oil on canvas, 38 x 56.5 cm

Gustave Courbet was one of the most important representatives of realism, a school of painting which chose to depict everyday reality and ordinary people instead of grand mythological or historical scenes.
This canvas, for example, represents a small area of beach with some rocks and a calm sea. There is no drama or even a human presence. However, the technique employed is spectacular: Courbet has applied the paint in broad sweeps using a palette knife. In several places the artist has left the canvas unpainted.
Van Gogh greatly admired Courbet and his work. He respected Courbet's attitude to art, for his refusal to paint subjects that did not exist. In one of his letters he agreed with Courbet's criticism of history paintings 'Peindre des anges! Qui est-ce qui a vu des anges?' (Paint angels! Who has ever seen an angel?) [522/418].

Gustave Courbet 1819–1877

View of the Mediterranean at Maguelonne, 1858

Oil on canvas, 92 x 135 cm

Harpignies was a realistic painter and contemporary of the impressionists. In 1869 chance brought him to the village of Hérisson, south of Bourges. He spent the summer in the Château de Montais, the country estate of one of his pupils. One day, while following a hunting party on horseback, he became lost and suddenly found himself face to face with the old castle of Hérisson, 'brightly lit against the background of a red-tinted, autumnal hillside'. Two years later he painted the castle ruins, their irregular silhouette sharply defined against the clear sky.

Harpignies' great hero was Camille Corot (1796–1875), the father of French realistic landscape painting. But while Corot produced subtle atmospheric effects in his landscapes, Harpignies' work is characterised by a more schematic approach and a pronounced chiaroscuro (distribution of light and dark).

Henri-Joseph Harpignies 1819–1916

79   **View of the Château d'Hérisson, 1871**

Oil on canvas, 41.2 x 63.5 cm

Claude Monet visited the Netherlands three times. During his first visit in the summer of 1871, he chose to stay in Zaandam, which was then a tourist attraction. The painter thought Zaandam 'all very amusing. Houses in all colours, mills by the hundred and delightful boats, exceptionally friendly Hollanders who almost all speak French. There is enough to paint for an entire lifetime', he wrote to his friend Camille Pissarro (1830–1903). Monet set to work with a passion and produced no less than 24 landscapes.

Mills in the Westzijderveld near Zaandam depicts the polder landscape to the west of Zaandam with its many characteristic sawmills and their adjacent sheds. The sails are fitted with summer canvases, typical of the region around Zaandam; these were used in the period from May to October. The painting is a fine example of the looser, experimental style that Monet developed around 1870.

Claude Monet 1840–1926
Mills in the Westzijderveld near Zaandam, 1871
Oil on canvas, 47 x 73.5 cm

In 1870 Dutch-born Alma-Tadema settled in London where he increasingly specialised in idealised scenes from classical antiquity. The painter rapidly acquired an international reputation, selling his work for astronomical prices. Alma-Tadema's paintings are characterised by intricate detail and a fine technique in which brush-strokes are barely visible. A greater contrast with Van Gogh's expressive style of painting could scarcely be imagined.

Alma-Tadema's figures radiate serenity; there is a total absence of drama or intense emotion. This is evident in *Our corner*, a work in which the painter portrayed his two daughters, Anna (born 1867) and Laurence (born 1865, standing in the painting). The girls are posing in one of the rooms in Townshend House, the family's London residence.

81

Lawrence Alma-Tadema 1836–1912

Our corner (portrait of Laurence and Anna Alma-Tadema as children), 6 October 1873
Oil on panel, 56.5 x 47 cm

From 1874 Puvis de Chavannes and eleven other artists worked on the decorations for the Panthéon in Paris. Murals many metres high were to depict scenes from the life of St Genevieve, patron saint of the French capital. Between 1874 and 1878 Puvis de Chavannes produced various studies of Genevieve's childhood. This work depicts a scene in which the young girl kneels in prayer, watched by several Gauls who would later become her protégés. Puvis explained that he intended to represent various levels of reality, with Genevieve's almost supernatural appearance counterbalanced by the astonished peasants. Van Gogh admired Puvis' work which he described as 'a strange meeting, by providence ordained, between long flown Antiquity and rough modern times' [878/614a].

Pierre Puvis de Chavannes 1824–1898

82   **Saint Genevieve as a child in prayer, c. 1874–76**

Oil on paper on canvas, 136.5 x 76.2 cm

This painting reflects the close working relationship between Camille Pissarro and Paul Cézanne (1839–1906). From 1872 the two artists lived and worked in the vicinity of Paris – Pissarro in Pontoise and Cézanne in nearby Auvers-sur-Oise. They painted with each other from 1873 onwards, creating an artistic dialogue in the form of landscapes and flower still lifes.

Pissarro painted mock orange, grass, honeysuckle, irises and peonies, which were his wife's favourite flowers. He appears to have produced this bouquet in two sessions: in the foreground he has clearly painted over the original green ground with red paint, while sections of the background and the bouquet itself have also been overpainted. After the first session Pissarro had apparently regarded the still life as complete, for he had already signed the work. His signature can be partly seen beneath the red paint in the foreground.

Camille Pissarro 1830–1903

83   **Still life with peonies and mock orange, 1872–74 and 1876–77**

Oil on canvas, 81 x 64.5 m

Flower still lifes

became a popular subject for several realist and impressionist painters during the 19th century, being admirably suited to experimentation with colour, light and form. Monticelli was also interested in this genre. His flower still lifes are characterised by a rich impasto (thickly applied paint) and the use of vigorous colour combinations. The artist painted this bouquet with short, thick brushstrokes. The flowers and the vase are composed of dabs of colour; with the exception of the forget-me-nots most of the flowers cannot be easily identified. Critics of Monticelli's work deplored the painter's loose technique. Van Gogh, however, did not agree with them for he admired Monticelli.

In 1886, the year Monticelli died, Theo van Gogh bought this flower still life for his own collection. Vincent wrote of this work: 'in terms of colour it is something of the first order' [830/617].

Adolphe Monticelli 1824–1886
Flower still life, c. 1875
Oil on panel, 51 x 39 cm

Seurat became famous for the development of pointillism, a style of painting with small dots of vibrant colour. He is best known for his monumental pointillist canvases such as *Bathers at Asnières* (1883–84, National Gallery, London) and *Sunday at La Grande Jatte* (1884–86, Art Institute of Chicago). Alongside his large canvases he made many small paintings and studies on wooden panels. These panels fitted exactly into the lid of his paint box, allowing him to paint outdoors and record impressions with ease. This work is an example of such a study, painted on the banks of the river Seine, just outside Paris.

Van Gogh called Seurat the leader of the painters of the 'Petit boulevard'. He used this term, that he had invented himself, to distinguish the younger generation of painters, including himself, from the 'Impressionnistes du Grand boulevard' such as Claude Monet (1840–1916), Edgar Degas (1834–1917) and Auguste Renoir (1841–1919).

Seurat's influence on Van Gogh is undeniable for he experimented with the same subjects, techniques and range of colours. Although Van Gogh would later develop his own style, he continued to admire Seurat's work.

Georges Seurat 1859–1891
Seine at Courbevoie, 1883–84
Oil on panel, 15.5 x 24.5 cm

Like the other impressionists Monet was deeply interested in the effects of light at various times of day. He wrote: 'To me a landscape barely exists, because its appearance changes constantly; it lives by the grace of its environment – the air and the light change ceaselessly'. His intention was to present an impression of the landscape which captured that aspect of its appearance determined by light. In this painting too, Monet has focused on the play of light. The work depicts a fleeting moment on a summer's day, with a coast road in full sunlight in the foreground and a blue-shadowed hill in the background.

Although Monet's paintings met with little acclaim early in his career, his success was increasing by the time he produced *La Corniche, near Monaco*.

Claude Monet 1840–1926

La Corniche, near Monaco, 1884

Oil on canvas, 74.4 x 93 cm

Signac's earliest

works were greatly inspired by the impressionists. He visited exhibitions and art dealers' galleries in order to study their methods and colours. The influence of impressionism on his early work is evident in the technique and the modern subject of this painting.

Signac soon came into contact with Seurat who inspired him to adopt the pointillist technique a year after painting this work. Together Signac and Seurat would form the neo-impressionist vanguard. Van Gogh, who was a friend of Signac, valued the painter's impressionist works more than his neo-

impressionist pieces. He also had a high opinion of Signac as a person, and wrote of him in 1889: 'Seldom or never have I had a conversation with an impressionist with on both sides so little disagreement or unpleasant confrontation' [756/581].

Paul Signac 1863–1935

88

Railway junction near Bois-Colombes, 1885

Oil on canvas, 46.4 x 65 cm

Toulouse-Lautrec

derived many of his subjects from the Parisian world of entertainment: cafés, brothels, music halls and cabarets. This work is probably a portrait of his lover and fellow artist Suzanne Valadon (1865–1938). The title of the painting refers to the contents of the little red pot on the table, This was filled with perfumed rice powder or 'whitener', used by women of the period to create a fashionable pale skin tone.

Toulouse-Lautrec met Van Gogh, who was ten years older, in the studio of Fernand Cormon (1845–1924), where both were studying. Vincent saw this painting shortly before he left Paris for Arles and described the canvas as typical of Paris life. His brother Theo bought the work for their private collection for 150 francs.

Henri de Toulouse-Lautrec 1864–1901
89   **Young woman at a table, 'Poudre de riz', 1887**
Oil on canvas, 56 x 46 cm

Lhermitte acquired a reputation as a painter of peasant life. The subjects of his canvases include scenes such as sheep-shearing or bringing in the harvest. According to Van Gogh the secret of Lhermitte's art was that he 'knew the sturdy, severe workman's figure through and through and seized his motifs from the bosom of the people' [335/277]. Van Gogh had the same interest in peasant life and the French artist's work provided him with a major source of inspiration.

Lhermitte probably intended this enormous painting not only to present a relaxed rendering of a peasant family at rest but also to symbolise the three ages of man – youth, adulthood and old age. The old man in the foreground is equipped with a scythe, a traditional reference to (approaching) death. This symbolism and the artist's emphasis on the romantic, idyllic aspect of peasant life were widely appreciated during the late 19th century.

Léon Augustin Lhermitte 1844–1925

Haymaking, 1887

Oil on canvas, 216 x 264 cm

In April 1887 Gauguin travelled to Panama in the company of the artist Charles Laval (1862–1894). After several weeks they left for the idyllic island of Martinique, where they lived in a simple hut. Here Gauguin found the unspoiled, seductive surroundings for which he had been seeking. He drew and painted the picturesque islanders and was fascinated by the graceful movements of the women. However, the primitive living conditions took their toll. Gauguin was incapacitated by fever and dysentery, and returned to France in a weakened condition in November 1887.

Shortly after his arrival in Paris he met the Van Gogh brothers. They were so impressed by *Among the mangoes at Martinique*, which Gauguin had produced on Martinique, that they purchased the painting for their own collection. It was the most expensive acquisition the brothers would ever make.

Paul Gauguin 1848–1903

Among the mangoes at Martinique, 1887

Oil on canvas, 89 x 116 cm

Fantin-Latour was chiefly known as a painter of flower pieces, although he also produced several group portraits of impressionists such as Claude Monet (1840–1926), Auguste Renoir (1841–1919) and Edouard Manet (1823–1883). Despite his friendship with these painters and early interest in Japanese art, his work was more traditional than that of his impressionist contemporaries. Fantin-Latour did not work outdoors but picked the flowers he needed, arranging these in a vase in his studio. When he painted this work he concentrated on the relationship between the various tones and colours.

After 1870 Fantin-Latour concentrated on mythological subjects. However, these works lack the artistic quality of his still lifes. In a letter Van Gogh described Fantin-Latour as 'one of the most independent spirits of our time' [578/B1].

Henri Fantin-Latour 1836–1904
Still life with flowers, 1887
Oil on canvas, 72 x 60 cm

Redon generally portrayed symbolist ideas and concepts, although he occasionally painted more realistic subjects as well. However, even these works often had a deeper meaning, as is the case with this picture.

The artist painted this small street in the village of Samois on the river Seine, a place where the Redon family spent the summers of 1888 and 1889. Their first summer there was overshadowed by tragedy when Redon saw his friend Emile Hennequin, an influential critic and defender of his work, drown in the river. Archival research has established that this canvas dates from that fatal summer.

For Redon the empty village street symbolised a feeling of loss and desolation. His letters indicate that streets of old houses had a special meaning for him: 'Nowhere has nature left a clearer trace of the insignificance of the human condition than on those melancholy walls; how deserted and desolate it is'.

Odilon Redon 1840–1916
Village street in Samois, 1888
Oil on canvas, 42.9 x 31.3 cm

Gauguin painted a portrait of Van Gogh during the time he spent in Arles. While Van Gogh generally based his works on observation, Gauguin often painted his pictures from memory or used his imagination. This may have been the case with this work, as he produced the painting in November 1888 when no sunflowers were blooming.

Gauguin's picture is his only portrait of Van Gogh and offers a rare insight into their intense collaboration in the tiny studio at the yellow house in Arles.

When Van Gogh saw this painting for the first time, he thought that Gauguin had portrayed him as a lunatic. However, he later modified his opinion: 'Since then my face has brightened considerably, but it is really me, worn out and extremely tense, as I was then' [802/605].

Paul Gauguin 1848–1903
Van Gogh painting sunflowers, 1888
Oil on canvas, 73 x 91 cm

95

In 1888, following the
example of Japanese print makers,
Van Gogh initiated an exchange
of portraits with his artist friends
Emile Bernard and Paul Gauguin.
Although he intended Bernard
and Gauguin to produce a portrait
of each other, they both opted to
paint a self-portrait with a small
portrait of the other artist in the
background. Van Gogh's initiative
produced three magnificent paintings which include this work by
Gauguin. The inscription, Les misérables à l'ami Vincent, refers to
the novel Les misérables by Victor
Hugo, whose protagonist Gauguin
maintained was just as misunderstood as 'a contemporary impressionist' [697/GAC33]. Van Gogh
was particularly impressed by the
melancholy character of the painting. He described the shadows on
his friend's face as 'despondent
blue', and declared that Gauguin
looked ill and anguished in the
portrait [701/545].

95

Paul Gauguin 1848–1903

Self-portrait with portrait of Bernard, 'Les misérables', 1888

Oil on canvas, 45 x 55 cm

Maurice Denis jointly founded the group of symbolist painters known as the Nabis in 1888. The simple forms, colour planes and flowered frame of *The two sisters* are typical features of the decorative effect which the Nabis painters aimed to create. This painting also clearly shows that Denis, like Van Gogh, was inspired by Japanese prints. The canvas originally formed part of a larger painting, based on the play *L'intruse* (The intruder) by the Belgian playwright Maurice Maeterlinck, in which three sisters wait for death to arrive. Like the other painters in the Nabis group, Denis endeavoured to express an état d'âme, a state of mind, in his work. The unearthly blue-green colours in the sisters' faces emphasise their fear.

Maurice Denis 1870–1943

96   **The two sisters, 1891**
Oil on canvas, 40.5 x 32.5 cm

98

Emile Bernard met Van Gogh while the Dutch artist was living in Paris. After Van Gogh moved to Arles the two remained in contact through an exchange of letters in which they included sketches. The artists used this correspondence to keep each other informed of their work and exchange ideas.

Bernard regularly stayed in Brittany. He based himself in the village of Pont-Aven where he was inspired by both the landscape and the 'primitive' peasants in their traditional costumes. Together with Gauguin, who also worked in Pont-Aven, he developed a new style of painting, which employed large colour planes, intense colours and heavily accented contours. Traditional perspective and spatial modelling were replaced by decorative compositions.

Bernard painted this work in Pont-Aven. The picture shows how during the early 1890s the artist drew inspiration from the colours and painting technique used by Paul Cézanne (1839–1906).

Emile Bernard 1868–1941

Pont-Aven seen from the Bois d'Amour, 1892

Oil on canvas, 101 x 76 cm

Although Redon was sometimes dubbed the painter of 'the fantastic', the artist repeatedly stressed that his work was based on an intensive study of nature. After meticulous observation of the natural world Redon was, as he himself said, always 'overcome with an urge to create something imaginary.'

'Something imaginary' also features in this depiction of an unknown person. It is not a portrait in the sense of a likeness of the model, but a general evocation of someone with closed eyes. Redon believed that one of a painter's most noble tasks was to produce a good portrait.

The canvas was purchased in 1913 by Andries Bonger, Theo van Gogh's brother-in-law. He had become acquainted with Redon in 1891 and assembled an important collection of his work. Bonger also ensured that the artist's oeuvre became known in The Netherlands through exhibitions.

Odilon Redon 1840–1916
Yeux clos (Eyes shut) c. 1894
Oil on card, 45.5 x 36.5 cm

Van Gogh had a considerable influence on the work of a later generation of artists, including the Dutch painter Jan Sluijters. The inspiration he derived from Van Gogh's style and use of colour is evident in this canvas.

In 1904 Sluijters won the Prix de Rome with a work that was still traditional in subject and technique. The prize, a scholarship to study abroad, enabled him to spend some time in Paris where he painted *Two women embracing* in 1906. Back in the Netherlands the teachers at the Rijksacademie (State Academy of Art) were distressed by this painting which they regarded as 'a mistaken pursuit of popular new colour moods and raw passion'. They disapproved of 'the sad disregard of Beauty in the female forms, the seemingly magnificent but painful cruelty of the colours, the raw technique that mocks the material'. Sluijters' scholarship was not extended.

Jan Sluijters 1881–1957
Two women embracing, 1906
Oil on canvas, 92 x 62.5 cm

Rotterdam-born Kees van Dongen settled in Paris in 1899. Around 1904 he met fellow artists Henri Matisse (1869–1954), Maurice de Vlaminck (1876–1958) and André Derain (1880–1954). Together with these colleagues he would become known as a representative of fauvism, a movement whose painters derived their use of intense colours from Van Gogh. From 1910 Van Dongen painted large planes of colours and distinct contrasts. A trip to Morocco in the summer of that year led him to adopt a more schematic approach, as is evident in this work. The painting represents an almost life-size portrait of the wife of the artist Guus van Dongen-Preitinger (1878–1946), whom he married in 1910.

The canvas, which Van Dongen probably painted in 1911, is a fine example of early 20th-century modernism that was partially inspired by Van Gogh.

100

Kees van Dongen 1877–1968
Portrait of Guus Preitinger, the artist's wife, c. 1911
Oil on canvas, 146 x 114 cm

96

Quotations from Van Gogh's letters are accompanied in the text by references, in square brackets, to two editions of these letters. The first number refers to: Han van Crimpen and Monique Berends (eds.), *De brieven van Vincent van Gogh*, 4 volumes, The Hague 1990; the second number to: *Verzamelde brieven van Vincent van Gogh*, 4 volumes, Amsterdam and Antwerp 1973.

Selections of works
John Leighton

Texts
Van Gogh Museum staff and
Denise Willemstein

Preparation and adaptation
Denise Willemstein

Editing
Sjraar van Heugten, Marije Vellekoop,
Roelie Zwikker

Translation
Michèle Hendricks

Design
Studio Roozen, Amsterdam

Production
Josette van Gemert, Melchert Zwetsman

Publication
Van Gogh Museum Enterprises B.V.,
Amsterdam

Lithography
Nederlof Repro, Cruquius Heemstede

Printing and binding
Snoeck-Ducaju & Zoon N.V., Ghent, Belgium

ISBN: 90-6314-015-0

100 Masterpieces

All works with a V in their inventory number are from the collection of the Vincent van Gogh Foundation. All other works belong to the Van Gogh Museum with the exception of nos. 77, 87 and 92 which are on long-term loan from the Rijksmuseum in Amsterdam.

1: s 416 M/1990	51: s 48 V/1962
2: s 3 V/1962	52: s 166 V/1962
3: s 141 M/1977	53: s 29 V/1962
4: s 139 V/1962	54: s 36 V/1962
5: s 7 V/1962	55: s 31 V/1962
6: s 5 V/1962	56: s 124 V/1962
7: s 87 V/1962	57: s 189 V/1962
8: s 2 V/1962	58: s 51 V/1962
9: s 1 V/1962	59: s 168 V/1962
10: s 140 V/1962	60: s 49 V/196
11: s 8 V/1962	61: s 172 V/1962
12: s 59 V/1962	62: s 41 V/1962
13: s 158 V/1962	63: s 46 V/1962
14: s 13 V/1962	64: s 196 V/1962
15: s 144 V/1962	65: s 176 V/1962
16: s 11 V/1962	66: s 175 V/1962
17: s 122 V/1962	67: s 188 V/1962
18: s 17 V/1962	68: s 50 V/1962
19: s 94 V/1962	69: s 105 V/1962
20: s 15 V/1962	70: s 104 V/1962
21: s 183 V/1962	71: s 88 V/1962
22: s 20 V/1962	72: s 107 V/1962
23: s 57 V/1962	73: s 106 V/1962
24: s 19 V/1962	74: s 195 V/1962
25: s 18 V/1962	75: s 149 V/1962
26: s 164 V/1962	76: s 505 S/2001
27: s 197 V/1962	77: s 77 B/1991
28: s 115 V/1962	78: s 455 V/1996
29: s 114 V/1962	79: s 450 S/1995
30: s 116 V/1962	80: s 503 S/2001
31: s 16 V/1962	81: s 454 S/1966
32: s 23 V/1962	82: s 438 M/1993
33: s 82 V/1962	83: s 502 S/ 2000
34: s 65 V/1962	84: s 251 V/1960
35: s 21 V/1962	85: s 489 S/1998
36: s 125 V/1962	86: s 415 M/1990
37: s 22 V/1962	87: s 190 B/1999
38: s 184 V/1962	88: s 381 M/1986
39: s 27 V/1962	89: s 274 V/1962
40: s 39 V/1962	90: s 424 M/1991
41: s 25 V/1962	91: s 221 V/1962
42: s 146 V/1962	92: s 89 B/1991
43: s 37 V/1962	93: s 436 M/1992
44: s 30 V/1962	94: s 225 V/1962
45: s 28 V/1962	95: s 224 V/1962
46: s 117 V/1962	96: s 423 V/1991
47: s 32 V/1962	97: s 293 V/1969
48: s 47 V/1962	98: s 500 N/1999
49: s 67 V/1962	99: s 382 M/1987
50: s 40 V/1962	100: s 493 S/1999